Eco Alert!
RAINFORESTS

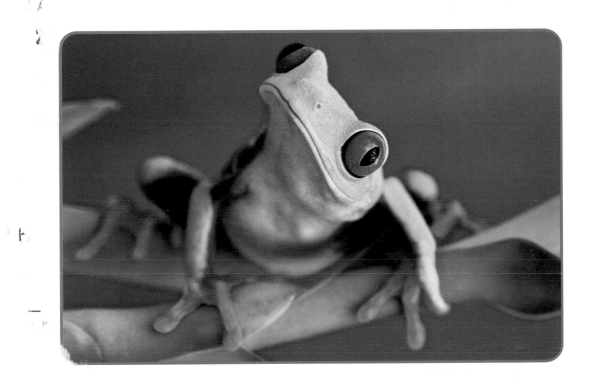

Rebecca Hunter

W
FRANKLIN WATTS
LONDON • SYDNEY

This edition 2012

First published in 2010 by
Franklin Watts
338 Euston Road
London NW1 3BH

Franklin Watts Australia
Level 17/207 Kent Street
Sydney NSW 2000

© 2010 Franklin Watts

ISBN 978 1 4451 0909 1

Dewey classification number: 333.7'514

A CIP catalogue record for this publication
is available from the British Library.

Planning and production by
Discovery Books Limited
Managing Editor: Rachel Tisdale
Editor: Rebecca Hunter
Designer: Blink Media
Picture research: Colleen Ruck
Illustrations: Stefan Chabluk

Printed in China

Franklin Watts is a division
of Hachette Children's Books,
an Hachette UK Company.
www.hachette.co.uk

Photographs: **Discovery Photo Library**: page 5
(Ed Parker/EASI-Images); **FLPA**: page 4 top (Gerry
Ellis/Minden Pictures), page 4 bottom (Michael
Krabs/Imagebroker), page 6 bottom (Matthias
Breiter/Minden Pictures), page 11 (Thomas
Marent/Minden Pictures), page 13 top (Albert
Visage), page 13 bottom (Cyril Ruoso/Minden
Pictures), page 15 (Konrad Wothe/Minden
Pictures); **Getty Images**: page 19 bottom
(Jaydirecto/Stringer), page 25 (Tim Graham), page
26 (Willard Clay), page 27 (Daniel Beltra), page 28
(Tim Laman), page 29 (Mark Warford/Stringer);
Istock: title page (Mark Kostich), page 18
(Iuoman); **Photodisc**: page 24; **Rebecca Hunter**:
page 19 right; **Shutterstock**: cover, foreground
(Harley Couper), background (szefel), page 4 top
(Orionmystery), page 8 (Trinh Le Nguyen), page 9
(L Barnwell), page 14 (Howard Sandler), page 16
(Carlos Neto), page 17 (Pichugin Dmitry), page 20
Frontpage), page 21 top (Jacek Chabraszewski),
page 21 bottom (Ronnie Howard), page 22
(Ella_K), page 23 (Charles Taylor).

Contents

Rainforests at risk

There is no other place in the world quite like a rainforest. From the leaf litter on the ground to the tops of the trees towering above, the forest is teeming with a fantastic display of plant and animal life.

On the floor of the forest amongst the ferns and **buttress** roots of the trees you will find thousands of species of insect, centipede, millipede and earthworm.

A few metres up, strangler figs and **lianas** coil their way around the tree trunks, creating aerial walkways for animals such as giant spiders, tree frogs, lizards and snakes.

High in the warm, wet layer of the **canopy** a multitude of flowers, fruits and seeds provide food for species including bats, birds and monkeys.

ⓐ Toucans live on the fruits of figs, palms and passion plants. Their continued existence is threatened by the destruction of the rainforests.

⊙ The rainforests of the world are being threatened as they are cut down and burned by people who want to use the land for other purposes.

The rainforest is a truly incredible **habitat** supporting an enormous wealth of life. But is this all about to be lost? In the distance strange noises can be heard. It is the sound of lorries and bulldozers making their way through the forest. It is followed by a deadlier noise, the sound of the chainsaw. Soon the trees will start falling. The plants that lived among them and the animals that lived on them will die. Many will die out completely as they are found nowhere else on Earth. The rainforests of the world are disappearing.

◉ The rainforest has an enormous diversity of plants, including many unique fern, liana, shrub and tree species.

What is a rainforest?

Rainforests are forests with tall trees, a warm **climate** and lots of rain. In most rainforests it rains nearly every day. There are two types of rainforest, tropical and temperate.

Tropical rainforests

Tropical rainforests are found around the equator between the **Tropics** of Cancer and Capricorn. They have rainfall between 1,500 and 2,500mm a year and the average temperature never drops below 18°C in any month.

Temperate rainforests

Temperate rainforests are found close to the ocean, usually on the west coast of continents. They have an annual rainfall of over 1,400mm and an average temperature of between 4 and 12°C.

⊕ Tortoise beetles are found in rainforests throughout the world.

⊕ Rainforests are hot or mild places with lots of rain. This stream flows through a temperate rainforest in Alaska, USA.

Central Africa holds the world's second largest tropical rainforest. The island of Madagascar, to the east of the continent, is home to many unique plants and animals found nowhere else on Earth.

The rainforests of Asia stretch from India and Burma in the west to Malaysia and the islands of Java and Borneo in the east.

⊙ This map shows the location of the tropical and temperate rainforests in the world. The forests once covered more than twice this area.

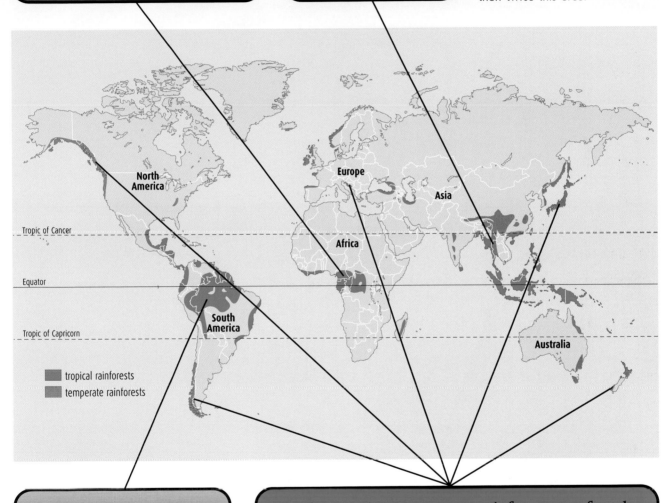

North America

Europe

Asia

Tropic of Cancer

Africa

Equator

South America

Tropic of Capricorn

Australia

■ tropical rainforests
■ temperate rainforests

The Amazon Basin contains the world's largest tropical rainforest. It is home to the greatest variety of plants and animals on Earth.

In the Americas, temperate rainforests are found between south-eastern Alaska and central California, and in Chile and the south of Argentina. They are also found in parts of Europe, Taiwan, China, Japan, south-eastern Australia and south-western New Zealand.

Rainforest destruction

People have been cutting down trees for hundreds of years, but the invention of **mechanised** cutting tools has made it easier and faster now than ever before. In the last 100 years, over half of the world's original 16 million square kilometres of rainforests have been destroyed.

Forests are not just damaged by the cutting down of trees. Heavy logging machines **compact** the ground, causing much of the soil to be washed away by **torrential** rain. Nothing will grow well on what is left.

Reasons for deforestation

There are two main reasons why people cut down trees. They either want the **timber** from the trees, or they want the land the trees grow on to use for something else.

Timber

Wood is one of the most useful natural materials. It has been used for centuries to make houses, ships, furniture, fences and many other products. The most valuable timber comes from rainforest trees. Slow-growing trees such as teak and mahogany produce an attractive wood that is much in demand. Wood also remains a main source of fuel for many people in **developing countries** around the world.

Farming

Worldwide, the greatest loss of rainforests has been due to the clearing of land for agriculture. Cattle ranching is one of the biggest destroyers of forests, especially in South America. In many cases, the grazing of the cattle damages the cleared land so badly that it is soon of no use to the ranchers any more. Eventually they move on, destroying more and more rainforest.

Forests are also cleared by farmers to grow crops such as sugar, maize, soya beans and coffee. These are called **cash crops** as they are exported abroad to bring money into the country.

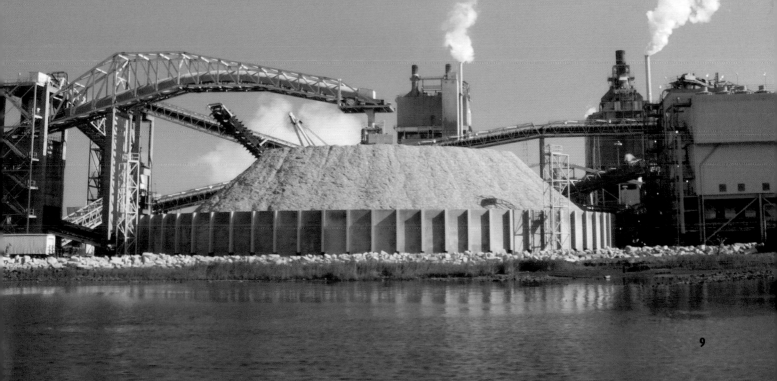

⊙ A paper pulp mill in Florida, USA. More and more rainforest is destroyed to meet the demands of the world's paper industry, which uses 200 million tonnes of wood each year.

The lungs of the world

The world's rainforests are often called 'the lungs of the world'. This is because they are very important in helping to control the balance of carbon dioxide (CO_2) and oxygen (O_2) in the atmosphere.

The carbon cycle

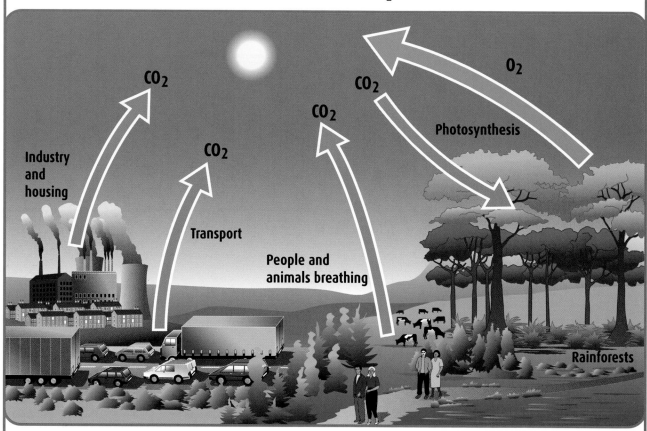

Industry and housing

CO_2

CO_2

Transport

CO_2

People and animals breathing

CO_2

Photosynthesis

O_2

Rainforests

Carbon is an **element** that is continually being recycled through animals, plants and the soil, and through the air as carbon dioxide. Trees take in carbon dioxide and give out oxygen during the process of **photosynthesis**. When they are cut down and burned, the carbon is released as carbon dioxide, increasing the levels of this gas in the atmosphere. Carbon dioxide is a greenhouse gas, which means it can add to **global warming** and may cause climate change.

Oxygen

Oxygen is an important gas that all living things need to **respire**. All the oxygen in the Earth's atmosphere is released by plants as they photosynthesise. Rainforests produce a massive amount of oxygen, which is moved around the Earth by wind systems. The Amazon rainforest alone produces more than 20 per cent of the Earth's oxygen.

Weather patterns

Rainforests also regulate temperatures and weather patterns worldwide. Much of the Sun's heat is **absorbed** by the dark surface of the rainforests. When they are cut down, this heat is reflected back into the atmosphere. The changes in temperature affect air currents in the atmosphere and can alter weather patterns thousands of kilometres away.

Water

Rainforests also act as an important water store. It is thought that one-fifth of the world's fresh water is in the Amazon Basin. The trees and soil act like a giant sponge, storing rainfall. They stop the rain running off the land and into rivers or sea. When trees are cut down, the water runs off the land causing floods and soil **erosion**.

⊙ Rainforests act like a giant air-conditioning system. They absorb the Sun's heat, store water, release huge amounts of cooling water vapour and, most importantly, remove a massive 4.8 billion tonnes of carbon dioxide from the atmosphere each year.

How can you help?

Help the atmosphere by planting a tree! One **broad leaf** tree will absorb around 1 tonne of carbon dioxide during its 100-year lifetime. Two fully-grown trees can provide enough oxygen for a family of four!

Rainforest plants

Rainforest plants come in an extraordinary variety of shapes and sizes, and are found in a range of levels in the forest.

Rainforest layers

The rainforest floor receives very little light so few plants grow here. It is hot and damp and the ground is covered in decomposing vegetation.

The **understorey** is also dark and **humid** and consists of shrubs, ferns and small trees. The small trees have to wait until an old tree falls down before they can get enough light to grow.

The rainforest canopy is made up of tall trees that grow to 30 or 40 metres high. Their **crowns** form a thick leafy layer that is home to a large number of animals.

Above the canopy a few taller trees poke out. This is the **emergent** layer. These trees can grow to heights of over 50 metres.

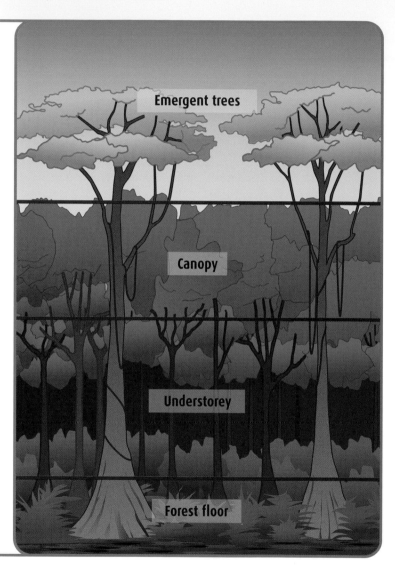

Emergent trees

Canopy

Understorey

Forest floor

Plant diversity

More than two-thirds of the world's plant species are found in rainforests. The Amazon alone is estimated to contain 80,000 species of flowering plants. The huge diversity of plant leaves, fruits, seeds and nuts means the rainforest can support a wide variety of animal species.

Medicinal plants

Many of today's medicines come from rainforest trees. The most important plant is probably the curare plant which is widely used as an **anaesthetic**. Quinine comes from the bark of the cinchona tree and has been used for many years to treat malaria. It is thought that about a quarter of all the medicines we use come from rainforest plants, and yet fewer than 1 in 10 plant species have been examined to see if they could be useful. As forests are cut down, many species become extinct before they have even been discovered.

The Rafflesia plant from Indonesia has the largest bloom of any flower and is one of the world's rarest and most endangered plants.

HOTSPOT:

Cancer-curing plant

The rosy periwinkle is a plant that is found only in the tropical rainforests of Madagascar. It contains a **compound** that can help treat children with leukaemia – a form of cancer. Children treated with this plant are now much more likely to survive the illness. The periwinkle is now cultivated (left) for this use.

Animals in the forest

Although rainforests only cover six per cent of the Earth's land surface, they have the highest **biodiversity** of any environment on Earth.

This is because rainforests provide an enormous number of habitats. They also have warm temperatures and high rainfall all year round, so there is always a plentiful supply of food and water and no harsh winter to survive. Different types of animals live in the rainforest layers.

HOTSPOT:

Endangered monkeys

The golden lion tamarin monkey (right) is found in the coastal lowland rainforests of Brazil. It is one of the most endangered of all rainforest animals. In the 1970s there were fewer than 200 of these small monkeys left, but after conservation efforts there are now about 1,500 living in the wild.

Animal diversity

The canopy is full of brightly-coloured birds, monkeys and sloths, while the understorey is home to frogs, lizards and snakes. Insects are found almost everywhere from the dark, damp forest floor, to the emergent trees where hundreds of species of butterfly dance in the sunshine.

Up in the canopy, Honduran white bats from Costa Rica make tents out of leaves. When light strikes the leaf, the white bats turn green and so are well-camouflaged.

Losing species

Many of the animals that live in the rainforest are already endangered. As more forests are cut down these species will die out completely. Scientists estimate that we are losing more than 137 species of plants and animals every day because of rainforest deforestation. Some rainforest species can only live in their natural habitat and will not survive in artificial habitats, such as zoos.

Bush meat trade

Many forest animals are also threatened by the bush meat trade. This is the killing of animals for people to eat. More than one million wild animals such as gorillas, chimpanzees and elephants are killed for their meat in the tropical forests of Africa each year.

Forest people at risk

People have lived by **hunting and gathering** in the rainforest for thousands of years. They hunt wild animals and gather plants, fruits and honey for food.

They use the forest resources to make tools, houses and boats, and to create medicines. When the forest people cut down trees to grow plants for food, they only clear tiny patches of rainforest. After a few years, they move on and the forest grows back. The people live in harmony with the forest.

But now other people want to use the rainforest. They clear vast areas of the forest to grow crops, ranch cattle, mine for minerals and build settlements. With the destruction of the forest for these activities, about 140 million forest people are in danger of losing their homes.

⊙ An Amazonian woman harvests bananas. Forest people have lived by hunting and gathering methods for centuries. Today they are under threat from the loss of their forest.

HOTSPOT:

The village that said 'No'

Big companies will pay huge sums of money for the rights to take the timber from the forests. But one village in Borneo, has said 'No' to the loggers. The village turned down a timber company's offer of US$300,000 for rights to their forest.

Instead they plan to go on living as they have always done: growing their own crops of rice and coffee, hunting for wild pigs and gathering **rattan** from the forest to sell.

Resettlement

In some countries, governments have tried to open up their rainforests to new populations. Both Brazil and Indonesia have encouraged settlers to live in the forests to try to reduce the population of their overcrowded city areas. These projects have not been a success. The new settlers do not have the same knowledge of the rainforest as the **indigenous** people. Once the valuable trees have been cut down and the soil fertility is lost, there is no way for these new settlers to earn money and live well in the forest.

Batwa dancers in Bwindi National Park, Uganda. The Batwa people are one of the oldest inhabitants of the forest and their way of life is under threat.

Logging the forests

Logging is the cutting down of trees for wood and wood products. Tropical hardwoods such as teak, mahogany and rosewood have been used for centuries to make houses, ships and furniture. Nowadays, timber is also wanted for paper-making, packaging, barbecue charcoal and fuel.

Clear-cutting

Clear-cutting is the cutting down of all the trees in an area. It is used to open up land for agriculture and ranching. Clear-cutting leaves land exposed to rain and then erosion. When the soil is exhausted and the farmers move on, a wasteland of **degraded** land is left.

HOTSPOT:

Temperate forest in danger

In Tasmania an average of 260 square kilometres of temperate rainforest is felled every year. The eucalyptus trees are cut and turned into woodchips for export to Japan, where they are processed into paper. Destruction of its habitat has left only 130 breeding pairs of the Tasmanian wedge-tailed eagle, which is now listed as an endangered species.

▶ An area of clear-cut rainforest in the Amazon. Cutting down trees in this way leaves the land exposed to erosion from wind and rain.

Selective cutting

When only a small amount of particular trees are wanted, the process of selective cutting should be a better method. But in fact the selective cutting process doesn't work very well either. As roads are built to carry the timber away, soil is compacted and **ecosystems** damaged. Studies have shown that when land is selectively cut, it will probably be clear-cut in the future.

Fragmentation

When selected trees are felled, they usually bring down a few other trees with them, making larger holes in the forest. Road construction breaks the forest up into smaller areas. This break-up of land is called fragmentation. When forest areas become fragmented, many animal species find it hard to survive. Their territories are too small for them to find enough food, shelter or mates to survive.

How can you help?

Don't buy wood products made from rainforest trees. The Forest Stewardship Council is an organisation that labels products which originate from well-managed, **sustainable** forests. Look for this logo on any wood products you buy.

◀ Many trees are cut down for use as fuel. Two billion people still depend on wood or charcoal for cooking and heating. This man is selling charcoal at a market in Manila in the Philippines.

19

Cattle ranching

Some people in the **western world** like to eat beef. Unfortunately much of this beef comes from countries that cut down rainforests to rear cattle.

Cattle ranching is the number one cause of deforestation in the Amazon Basin and in Central America. Since 1970, over 600,000 square kilometres of Amazon rainforest have been destroyed.

Destroying the soil

Ranching cattle is a very destructive use of land. At first the land is fertile and grass will grow. But the grasses quickly take **nutrients** from the soil and the land then has to be fertilised. Fertilisers may add nutrients to the soil, but they cannot hold it together. Before long, the churning of thousands of cattle hooves turns the soil to dust and heavy rains wash it away. The cattle ranchers abandon their ranches, buy more land, cut down more trees and raise more cattle. The once lush rainforest areas are left as barren wastelands.

⊙ Cleared rainforest land such as this in Brazil, can be grazed for five to seven years before the soil is exhausted and the land has to be abandoned.

Brazil's cattle market

In Brazil, about 80 per cent of deforestation is caused by cattle ranches. There are about 65 million beef cattle in Brazil, but the government wants to double its share of the world beef export market from 30 per cent to 60 per cent in the next decade. This will surely lead to the destruction of more rainforests.

◀ For every hamburger consumed from rainforest beef, about five square metres of forest is cleared.

How can you help?

Don't buy beef reared in rainforest areas. Check the labels at the supermarket and make sure you are buying beef that has been reared in your own country. It will reduce the **air miles** of your food too!

HOTSPOT:

Jaguars threatened

Jaguars (left) in the Pantanal region of Brazil are threatened by ranchers who shoot them because they prey on their cattle. However, a new tourism venture hopes to persuade the local people that these beautiful big cats are worth more alive than dead.

Clearing land for agriculture

Every year thousands of square kilometres of rainforest are destroyed for agricultural use. There are two main groups who are responsible for this – poor farmers and big companies.

Shifting cultivation

For centuries, forest people have cleared small sections of land to grow crops. After two or three years they move on and clear another patch. This method is called **shifting cultivation** and works quite well because the forest is cut down in small areas and has time to re-grow. But now many more people are moving into the forests along roads built by loggers. To clear the forest quickly, they use the **slash-and-burn** method to release the nutrients from the trees into the soil. Large numbers of these shifting cultivators are now causing extensive damage to the forest.

⊙ A view of an oil palm plantation. Palm oil is exported all over the world. Over one billion people consume it and it is found in one in ten supermarket products.

Big business

Forests are also cleared to grow single crops in an **intensive** way. These cash crops, such as sugar, soya beans, coffee, rubber and oil palm, cover huge areas of previously forested land. At present, coffee farms cover over 30,000 square kilometres of land in the northern parts of South America. In southern China about 67 per cent of the region's rainforests were lost to rubber plantations between 1976 and 2003.

Palm oil in Indonesia

Oil palm is the most productive oil seed in the world. The crop is very profitable when grown in large plantations. Indonesia's oil palm plantations grew to more than seven million hectares by 2009, and the government plan to develop even more in the future. As well as being used extensively in the food and pharmaceutical industry, a major use of palm oil is for **biofuels**. Drivers in the USA and Europe who want to fill their cars with 'green' fuel may be doing so at the expense of Indonesia's already threatened forests.

HOTSPOT:

Saving orangutans

In Borneo, the orangutan (below) is under serious threat from the oil palm industry. Adults are shot for raiding the palm trees and their babies are sold as illegal pets. The Borneo Orangutan Survival Foundation has saved over 600 orangutans. The babies need to be looked after for six years before they can be released in conservation areas.

Mining the rainforests

Rainforest areas are often rich in precious metals including copper, silver and gold. They may also contain minerals, such as aluminium and iron ore, or **fossil fuels**, such as oil and coal.

Mining the forest for these natural resources is very destructive. Huge areas of trees must be felled, and large access roads built to allow mining machinery in. Often the waste from the mines pollutes local rivers and kills wildlife.

HOTSPOT:

Mining in Madagascar

A nickel mine company is planning to tear up 15 square km of rainforest in Madagascar. The forest is home to over 1,300 species of flowering plants, 14 species of lemurs (right) and over 100 species of frog. The mining company has promised to minimise its impact by moving wildlife and replanting trees, but conservationists say many **endemic** species will become extinct.

Dangers of gold

The gold mining industry uses dangerous chemicals, such as cyanide and sulphuric acid, to extract gold. In Guyana in 1995, over three billion litres of cyanide-laced water was accidentally released into a river after a dam burst. This caused the widespread deaths of many aquatic plants and animals. The water supply that locals used for drinking and irrigating their crops was polluted for many months afterwards.

Iron ore in Brazil

An enormous iron ore mine in the north-east of Brazil has led to an area of forest bigger than France being destroyed. About 45 million tonnes of iron ore are processed each year, as well as large quantities of copper, manganese and gold. The iron smelters are fuelled with charcoal, which is made from trees from the surrounding forest. The iron produced by this project is exported, mainly for car manufacture in Japan and Europe.

The Carajas iron ore mine in Brazil has led to the destruction of huge areas of rainforest by the open-cast mines. However new towns and industries have been created in the area, providing work for thousands of people.

Save the rainforests!

All over the world people are uniting to save the rainforests. You can help in many ways both at home and by supporting projects and organisations that campaign on behalf of rainforests.

We have seen how you can have a small-scale effect by not eating rainforest beef and not buying rainforest wood products. Larger organisations can have an even bigger effect.

Stopping soya in the Amazon

Soya bean growth had become one of the main threats to the Amazon rainforest. The soya produced was being used to feed animals destined for fast-food chains in Europe and the USA. After massive consumer pressure, led by Greenpeace, McDonald's has said it will no longer use chickens fed on soya grown in deforested areas of the Amazon rainforest.

⊙ Soya beans have become one of the most important contributors to deforestation in the Brazilian Amazon.

▶ Environmental activists protest about the clear-cutting of a forest, leaving a solitary, protected Brazilian nut tree.

Paper waste

The WWF is campaigning to stop wasteful paper consumption. About one million tonnes of paper are used every day. Half of the trees cut down commercially end up in paper products.

Save the Sumatran rainforest

The RSPB (Royal Society for the Protection of Birds) is campaigning to save the Harapan rainforest in Sumatra. This forest is so rich in wildlife that it has been described as one of the world's 'biodiversity hotspots'. It contains at least 280 bird species and many rare amphibian, reptile and mammal species, including the Sumatran tiger, one of the world's rarest mammals.

How can you help?

Save trees by using less paper. Reuse and recycle what you can. Each tonne of recycled paper can save 17 trees!

We can all help save the rainforests by thinking 'TREES'!

| **T**each others about the importance of the environment and how they can help save rainforests. | **R**estore damaged ecosystems by planting trees on land where forests have been cut down. | **E**ncourage people to live in a way that doesn't hurt the environment. | **E**stablish parks to protect rainforests and wildlife. | **S**upport companies that operate in ways that minimise damage to the environment. |

The future for rainforests

It is unfortunate that nearly all of the world's tropical rainforests are located in some of the poorest countries in the world. These countries want food to feed their people, and need to export items to make money.

It is easy to see why these countries want to exploit their own resources. But there are ways in which the forests could be saved that would satisfy everyone.

Global funds

One suggestion is that a global multibillion-dollar fund should be set up to pay the owners of the world's rainforests not to cut them down. This would not only save the forests, but also reduce greenhouse gas emissions, and give vital money to the developing countries.

Ecotourism

Ecotourism, where tourists are encouraged to visit endangered places, is another way of making money from the natural forest. If local people can make money from ecotourists coming to see their animals and plants, they won't be so keen to destroy them.

⊙ Ecotourism has become an important way of preserving the rainforests. By constructing aerial walkways and bridges, ecotourists can see many rainforest species at different levels of the forest.

A profitable future

If governments, landowners and those living in the rainforest were given a good reason not to destroy the rainforest, it could be saved. If the forest was used as a supply of medicinal plants, fruits, nuts, oils and other resources such as rubber, chocolate and chicle (used to make chewing gum), the trees would be saved and money would be made. Rainforest users make around $150 per hectare for cattle ranching and $990 per hectare out of timber. But if the forest was harvested sustainably, nearly $6,000 could be made per hectare from forest products.

Saving the Great Bear

The Great Bear rainforest in Canada is the largest intact, coastal temperate rainforest left in the world, and has recently achieved a new protection status. The government has reached an agreement with logging industries to develop a conservation-based economy in the region. This will ensure that an estimated 108 million tonnes of CO_2 remain locked up in its standing trees.

⊙ A member of the environmental group Greenpeace chains himself to logging equipment as part of a protest against clear-cutting the Great Bear rainforest in British Columbia, Canada.

Glossary

Absorbed
Taken in by something.

Air miles
The distance travelled by goods by air in order to be sold.

Anaesthetic
A drug that reduces pain.

Biodiversity
The range of living things present in an area.

Biofuels
Fuels, such as biodiesel or methane, made from living things.

Broad leaf
Trees with large, green leaves.

Buttress
Thick roots that flare out from the base of tall, rainforest trees.

Canopy
The top layer of vegetation in a forest.

Cash crops
Crops that are grown to be sold for money.

Climate
The average weather in a region over a period of years.

Compact
To pack down soil by vehicles or equipment.

Compound
A chemical made by the combination of two or more other chemicals.

Crown
The very top of a tree.

Degraded
Broken down or showing a decline in quality.

Developing countries
Poorer countries where people have a low standard of living and low levels of industry.

Ecosystems
A group of living things together with the place in which they live and the food they depend on.

Element
A substance made up of just one type of atom.

Emergent
A forest tree that stands taller than the trees around it.

Endemic
Occurring naturally only in a single geographical area.

Erosion
The wearing away of rock or soil by the action of water or wind.

Fossil fuels
Fuels including coal, oil and natural gas that were formed underground millions of years ago.

Global warming
A rise in the average temperature of the Earth which many people think is caused by an increase of greenhouse gases in the atmosphere.

Habitat
The natural conditions in which a plant or animal lives.

Humid
Having a high level of moisture in the air.

Hunting and gathering
A way of living that involves getting wild food from the environment.

Indigenous
A species which is native to a particular region.

Intensive
A way of farming that produces a lot of crops or animals in a small area.

Liana
A woody, climbing, tropical vine.

Mechanised
Equipment that requires a motor.

Nutrients
Food or chemicals that plants and animals need to grow.

Photosynthesis
The process by which green plants make energy from sunlight, water and carbon dioxide.

Rattan
A tropical plant that is used in wickerwork.

Respire
To breathe air in and out.

Shifting cultivation
A way of farming where farmers regularly move their cultivated land to another area.

Slash-and-burn
A type of farming in which the ground is cleared by cutting and burning the vegetation.

Sustainable
Exploiting the natural resources without destroying the environment or depleting a resource.

Timber
The wood in trees that is available for use.

Torrential
Falling fast and in great quantities.

Tropics
The area on the Earth between the Tropic of Cancer and the Tropic of Capricorn.

Understorey
The layer of vegetation in a forest below the canopy but above the ground.

Western world
Developed countries that are wealthy and have a high standard of living.

Further information

Books

Rainforest (Up Close)
Paul Harrison, Franklin Watts, 2009

Rainforest Destruction (What If We Do Nothing?)
Ewan McLeish, Franklin Watts, 2007

Rainforests in Danger (Earth SOS)
Jenny Vaughn, Franklin Watts, 2007

Vanishing Forests (Green Alert!)
Lim Geng Puay, Raintree Publishers, 2004

Rainforests at Risk (Precious Earth)
Jen Green, Chrysalis Children's Books, 2003

Websites

http://kids.mongabay.com
This site has all you need to know about rainforests. Why are rainforests important? Why are rainforests disappearing? How can we save rainforests?

www.rainforestsos.org
The Prince's Rainforests Project was set up by HRH The Prince of Wales to promote awareness of the urgent need to take action against tropical deforestation.

www.worldwildlife.org/what/wherewework/amazon/index.html
Learn all about the world's largest rainforest at the World Wildlife Fund. Explore their conservation projects in action today.

www.worldlandtrust.org
Help save the rainforest with the World Land Trust. Your donation can directly help save an area of rainforest.

Note to parents and teachers: Every effort has been made by the publishers to ensure that these websites are suitable for children and that they contain no inappropriate or offensive material. However, because of the nature of the Internet, it is impossible to guarantee that the contents of these sites will not be altered. We strongly advise that Internet access is supervised by a responsible adult.

Index